IO KEYS TO EFFECTIVE TIME MANAGEMENT FOR TEENS

A Practical Handbook for Busy Teenagers to Accomplish Their Goals and Pursue Their Passion Projects

Tori Senior

DAYELight
PUBLISHERS

ISBN: 978-1-958443-63-7 (paperback)

Scripture quotations marked "KJV" are taken from the Holy Bible, King James Version (Public Domain).

Scripture quotations marked "ESV" are from the ESV Bible® (The Holy Bible, English Standard Version®), copyright © 2001 by Crossway Bibles, a publishing ministry of Good News Publishers. Used by permission. All rights reserved.

I dedicate this book to my grandmothers, who were here when I started this journey but are now in a better place. They always encouraged me, and I know they would have been very proud of me.

ACKNOWLEDGMENTS

I want to thank my book coach, Crystal Daye, for helping me along this journey. She guided and motivated me to keep going no matter what.

I am grateful to my parents, who have invested in opportunities to help me produce this book.

I want to acknowledge all the other family members, friends, and anyone else who has encouraged me along this journey.

Finally, I want to thank God for helping me to never give up, even when I felt like giving up on this book.

I hope you will enjoy this book and learn something from it.

TABLE OF CONTENTS

INTRODUCTION

BUSY ME

At fourteen, what makes me qualified to write this book? After all, teens aren't that busy, or so many people like to think. I am sure most, if not all, teens can agree with me and say that teens are very busy. As a swimmer, violinist, coder, top student, and author—the list goes on—I know a thing or two about time management. Oh, and not to mention the constant chores and keeping up with assignments, especially the dreaded group projects. In fact, in the week I started writing this chapter, I had five group projects (and a few other graded assignments) due. God knows that if I couldn't manage my time, I wouldn't be keeping up with all the tasks that demand my attention.

Sometimes, I get so busy that I leave no room for a relationship with God. The fact is, I am just at the beginning of my teenage years, so I may not know entirely how teenagers can manage their time well to be effectively productive. However, I have been a busy child my entire life. Entering my teenage years with these responsibilities has taught me a lot. The purpose of this book is to share that knowledge.

A teenager is the middle ground between an adult and a child, so you are still learning a lot about life, and you have a lot of schoolwork. You probably have a grand idea for a business but no time or knowledge about how to start it. You are required to do menial tasks like washing dishes and cleaning and not-so-menial tasks like cooking. Balancing a social life and school while trying to explore other avenues of life, like business or sports, can get hectic.

Often, teenagers sacrifice their sleep as the first resort to get everything done. Research shows that this just makes matters worse. As a teenager, your brain is in its prime stage of development, and losing sleep only stunts your brain growth. Sleep and any other type of rest, in general, are necessary to get tasks done and should not be sacrificed to get them done. As for me, if I have an assignment that I somehow left until the last minute and it is getting late and I am tired, I will go to sleep and wake up early to finish it. It is not worth it to lose sleep for sub-standard work that is going to take longer to do because I am tired. Of course, if I had managed my time a little better, that situation could have been avoided.

Not only am I going to help you manage your time, but I want to teach you what to do when you run out of time (only as a last resort). Come to think of it, the stress you experience when the clock is ticking—time is running out; you are tired; you have other work to do; you probably haven't eaten yet—isn't a good mix.

The ten keys to time management for teens that I will be referring to in this book should help you live your teenage years with less stress and allow you to accomplish all you want to.

To those who have said with all the advice I give, I could write a book, well, here it is.

I

SCHEDULING

"Productivity is never an accident. It is always the result of a commitment to excellence, intelligent planning, and focused effort."

—Paul J. Meyer

A schedule should not make your life rigid. It should allow you to break your tasks into smaller pieces that are easier to manage than the big task at hand. Often, it is thought that a schedule only means deciding what to do at each point in the day, but I believe a schedule is not only that. It means you go into each day knowing what you want to accomplish and how you plan to accomplish it. It means that when you wake up in the morning, you don't feel bored because you have "nothing" to do and just scroll and catch up on the lives of others. It means that the "nothing" you must do is transformed into something.

There is always something to do, and many times in life, we don't want to do what needs to be done or know where to start. Telling yourself to just do it at a different time because it is too big to tackle is not the solution. It usually ends in that task feeling bigger than before and you rush to do it at the "11th hour."[1] Think of it like this: every big task can be broken down into smaller, more manageable tasks. Just writing a to-do list that says "Read literature book" is not going to make you do it. I am sure that the literature book is not one big chapter. You can break it into parts like "Read chapter 1 and identify main characters," "Read chapter 2 and identify the themes in the first two chapters," etc. This can be spread across a period, and it not only looks but feels like you are getting more done.

One of my favourite quotes is one by Lao Tzu that says, *"The journey of a thousand miles begins with a single step."* This can be applied to any aspect of life, whether it be schoolwork, a passion project, learning a language, etc. However, what is key to note is that you just need to start, and it is easier to start when you know where to start and how to

---

[1] '11th hour' refers to the last possible moment you could do something before you no longer have the opportunity. Essentially, you're almost out of time.

proceed once you have started. Breaking up a large task into smaller tasks makes it easier to know where to start as you have simpler tasks to tackle.

Breaking up your day into segments with individual tasks allows you to get more done without the hassle of trying to figure out what to do. Have you truly thought about the time you take up in a day trying to figure out what to do or what to do first? Sometimes you settle for not doing anything at all. You must at least know what you are going to do before you attempt to do it so it doesn't end in chaos. You must at least know how you are going to do what you are going to do before you do it.

Everyone has the same 24 hours in a day; it is how you spend it that makes the difference. Taking fifteen minutes every night to write down what you are going to do the next day could make all the difference. If you want a plainer view of what to do, identify the time in the day that you will do certain tasks. But to do that, you must know how your body operates. For example, if you are more focused early in the morning, that might be a good time to try and study. If your brain is more creative early in the morning, that might be a good time to do art if you like art or channel that creativity into a passion project or a business idea that you came up with. I

15

personally feel more productive and driven early in the morning, so I do schoolwork at that time and work on my passion project later in the day, making sure to make note of any ideas I get throughout the day. Additionally, when it gets to a certain point in the day, it would take brute force to get myself to do schoolwork. Not everyone's body works like mine, so I can't tell you exactly how to align your day to maximize your productivity. Everyone's body works differently, so you must learn how your body works so you can maximize the different points in the day to develop a skill that time will cater to the most.

School takes up a lot of time in the day, but you must learn to put school into your schedule rather than make your schedule around school. This means your life does not fully revolve around school. The time you wake up is not based on what time school starts and how long it takes for you to get ready but rather on what you want to accomplish when you wake up, including the time it takes you to get ready for school.

When you want to accomplish a goal that is unrelated to school, you must make time to dedicate to that goal outside of school. You will not accomplish that goal if you do not make time to accomplish it. Take a moment to think how much easier it would be to finish a project in a week if you broke the project down into parts and worked on a part each day. Take a moment to think about how much easier it would be to study for a test if every time you learnt something new, you went home and tried to review and understand it. Every once in a while, you go back to it so that the day before the test, you already understand the topic, and you don't need to try to relearn it or just learn it because you didn't grasp it when it was originally taught.

As teens, we often complain so much about how much work we must do and never try to think of a way to make that work seem less. No doubt, a lot is required of you to do, and a lot is there to do, but complaining instead of trying is not going to make the situation any better. We can waste a lot of time looking at the problem in front of us and never actually try to solve it.

> *"Productivity is never an accident. It is always the result of a commitment to excellence, intelligent planning, and focused effort."*
> —*Paul J. Meyer*

The only way you can get where you want to be is to keep trying daily, no matter how much you want to give up. Plan every day to try again with what you want to achieve. Occasionally, there will be times when it will be hard to try, but you must keep trying.

> *"You always pass failure on your way to success."*
> —*Mickey Rooney*

It is what you do with the failure that decides whether you succeed or not. You must decide when you fail, if you are going to be upset about it, or if you are going to learn from it and use it to succeed. Scheduling will help you to keep yourself accountable for what you must do and ensure you do it. It is not just a rigid daily timeline; it is a focused effort to continue trying that will eventually lead to your success.

You must keep trying if you want to achieve success, and scheduling keeps you trying. It makes you get up every day to do a task you may not have wanted to do and to keep doing it until you reap the results and benefits.

When you are scheduling, there are mistakes you can make. Firstly, never make your schedule in such a way that it is not flexible because you don't have total control over your life. The aim is to always be so far ahead of 'deadlines' that if there is an emergency, you can reschedule. But this shouldn't be used as an excuse for procrastination. In essence, you should schedule with the aim of following the schedule but be able to adjust it if something comes up.

Secondly, your rest time should also be scheduled. Rest is any activity that is not demanding and is often an enjoyable task. It is better defined as *"ceasing work or movement in order to relax, sleep or recover strength."* In this way, you can rejuvenate your mental, physical or social 'battery.' According to Dr. Saundra Dalton-Smith, there are seven types of rest: physical, mental, emotional, social, sensory, creative, and spiritual. She also says that if we find ourselves exhausted after resting, it may mean that we are missing out on one of these types of rest. Not scheduling rest is an easy way to lead to burnout. Furthermore, when you don't schedule rest and get burnt out, you use that as an excuse to rest for an indefinite amount of time.

Not scheduling rest can also lead to sporadic breaks. A sporadic break is when you take a break at any time during your schedule because you feel like you are getting bored or tired of following your schedule. This can lead to wasting time and taking a while to get back on task.

Lastly, a schedule can be used to build habits. It's not meant to lead a monotonous lifestyle. A schedule is used for structure, not repetitiveness. When you first make a schedule, you want to include every single daily habit you would like to implement, along with other various daily activities. After a while, those practices become embedded subconsciously into that point in the day, so it is almost impossible not to do them at that point in the day. When those habits are on your schedule, you do them, so don't overlook putting simple tasks on your schedule. When those practices become habits, it may not be necessary to have them on your schedule anymore because they are ritualistic. You are then able to focus more on other activities that can't necessarily be habitual.

When you don't have any form of structure or good habits in your day, it is necessary to put simple tasks on your schedule. When you build these habits and doing them becomes natural, you can then revert to a more to-do-list type of scheduling. This is when you write down your aims for that day. When you have that awareness about how your body works and what task is best to do at what point in the day, you will eventually know what to do because you are already aware of what time in the day is most beneficial for each task.

Don't let anything deter you from having a structured schedule. In the end, it is what works best for you. As much as you can schedule, it will not work if you don't follow it.

2

PRIORITISE, DON'T PROCRASTINATE

"Procrastination is the art of keeping up with yesterday and avoiding today."

—*Wayne Dyer*

Procrastination leads to more stress. We have established how scheduling can help us manage our time better, but what happens when we procrastinate and it all comes down to the wire[2]? You should know what is more important at a certain time. You have the ability to prioritise what is more important. This doesn't mean you drop everything else, but you should know what to dedicate the most time to in your schedule based on what is most crucial at that point in time.

---

[2] 'All comes down to the wire' means that there is little time left.

Many people have a habit of having something critical to do that they don't want to do, so they suddenly remember another task that is trivial and use that as an excuse as to why they couldn't do the necessary task. Why is it that when you have a test in two days, you suddenly remember that you have a dirty room and decide to deep clean it? It is likely that you were told to clean that room several times before but, at that point in time, you would rather do it than study. The point is that cleaning your room is not the most crucial task at that moment, and inevitably, you need to study for that test. It would be better if you had more than one night to study for it. Remember what I said in the previous chapter about splitting up a task when you get it so you can tackle it a little bit each day? When you don't do this, the best way to tackle the tasks at hand is to prioritise.

The reality is, every day, the list of things to do gets longer, and whatever you put off from the previous day gets carried over into the next day. As a result, you have more to do in a day than the number of hours you have to do it. This leads to sacrificing sleep to get it done, which is not a good thing. I will discuss more in the next chapter why sacrificing sleep isn't good, but as of right now, we can be satisfied with the fact that it is not. I get it; you have a lot to do, and sometimes you just don't get the chance to do those tasks, but you have to know what is more important. This often includes sacrificing social functions and relaxation time to get important tasks done. This, in no way, should indicate that you should always be busy with a new task, but you should have the wisdom to decide when you can take a break and when you can't. This could mean saying no to going out with your friends to stay home and work on your part of the group project that is due soon or sacrificing a little of your extra time to review a concept for your upcoming test that you don't fully understand. This doesn't mean you should not rest; it is all about balance. It is a good practice to make appointments with yourself, and you know that nothing should interfere with that set time. This is similar to when you set a doctor's appointment. You have to get there at the time specified so you try your best, despite all circumstances, to show up at the time agreed on. It is easier to make the time for the doctor's appointment because someone else is relying on you to be there. However, we should be able to keep these same promises to ourselves. It may be useful to ask someone else to keep you accountable for the promises you make to yourself. This is more commonly known as having an 'accountability partner.' You both ensure that you keep each other accountable for promises you made to yourself.

How prioritisation works can vary depending on how far away the "due date" is for the task, the size of the task, whether you are working on it with others or on your own, and how much you already know about things that relate to the task. Let's say, for example, you must learn a music piece to perform Sunday evening and it is now Wednesday morning. You will be playing this piece alone, and you must find the music for the piece yourself based on a topic you were given. You haven't started learning the song yet, but you have found the music for it. Not only that, but you haven't played that instrument in a while, so you are slightly "rusty." In this case, you have five days to prepare, including Sunday morning after church with your family, and you have a lot of practice to do. You first need to ensure that you can play your instrument properly and then practice the piece you have to play. Realistically, practicing that instrument is not the only thing you have to do for five consecutive days. You would, more than likely, have other important things to do. You could possibly have a test the Friday before that you know a good amount about, but you still see the need to study for. The procrastinator mindset would tell you to leave the music practice until Saturday and focus 100% on studying for that test. This may not seem like procrastinating, but it is. You want to believe that you are being productive because the test comes first, but truly you are not prioritising your time well. When it is time to practice that instrument on Saturday, you may want to trick yourself into thinking that you had a very hectic week and you need some sleep so you can practice the instrument later. The truth is, when you practice it later, in order to allow the music to be as good as is necessary to perform the following day, you would have to practice for hours as a result of not having any prior practice. Plus, you would get less sleep because you stayed up practicing. Furthermore, you would not only be tired the following day from a lack of sleep, but you would be extra stressed over the fact that you did not get enough time to practice. The best way to handle this from Wednesday would have been to split your time between studying and practicing. Spend 60% of your time studying and 40% practicing, and then after the test, you can spend 100% of your time practicing in order to prepare for your performance. In this case, you would be prepared for your test by Friday because you already know most of the information. You would have been much better at playing your instrument and probably be able to at least start learning the piece for your performance.

Prioritisation doesn't just mean you do what is needed first at the beginning. It also means analysing how much time is necessary to be split among a group of tasks to reap the best benefits from each, no matter how much time you have left. The best thing to do is split up your tasks the moment you get them, but you have to know which task is more important and which tasks demand more time, whether they come first or not. Procrastination might allow you to relax for a time, but when "push comes to shove,"[3] all hell breaks loose. Therefore, prioritise your time effectively and in accordance with all factors at play. This way, you can decide which task requires the most time at a single moment.

---

[3] 'Push comes to shove' means you have no other choice but to do that task.

3

GET ENOUGH SLEEP

"Sleep is an investment in the energy you need to be effective tomorrow."

—*Tom Rath*

When you think about getting enough sleep, it is not only important to think about how much sleep you are getting but the quality of sleep you are getting. The Centre for Disease Control and Prevention (CDC) states that teenagers should get eight to ten hours of sleep. This is not generally the case. Many teens I meet don't get even close to enough sleep. Some consider six hours of sleep a gift. Furthermore, many research sites support my point that teens don't get as much sleep as they need. What many people usually say is that they have too much work. It is one of the most classic excuses a teen can give.

Check your screen time. Evaluate what you spend your hours on during the day. Think back to see how much time you truly dedicate to certain activities. As I said previously, you have a lot to do, but you should never use it as an excuse. Life gets easier when you change your mindset and realise that it is not about how much work you have but how you split your time to get it done. The mismanagement of time leads to many teens being up at night trying to do schoolwork that they could have done earlier. This eventually leads to sleep deprivation. Research shows that sleep deprivation is a terrible thing and can lead to an increased risk of hypertension, obesity, depression, heart attack, and stroke. Sleep deprivation also leads to reduced alertness, shortened attention span, poor memory, reduced concentration, slower reaction time, and more, according to the National Institutes of Health and betterhealth.vic.au.gov.

Sleep deprivation affects school performance and stunts physical and mental growth. Not only can mismanagement of time lead to sleep deprivation, but a result of sleep deprivation is poor performance. It is a vicious cycle. Too much of anything is not good for you. Yes, I said it. Too much sleep, too much work, too much play, and too much rest are not good for you. You must have a healthy balance. You can't work all day. You can't play all day. You can't sleep all day. Peace is restored when you get enough sleep. This brings balance to your daily routine.

I have seen the consequences of not getting enough sleep and the benefits of getting enough sleep. Sleep allows you to look and feel healthier. You also perform better in school because of the increased concentration and better memory. Think about it, if you change your work-to-rest ratio from 1:9 (10% work and 90% rest), with rest not being the sleep you get but activities you do to relax or unwind, to at least 5:5 (50% each), you would be able to spend less of your sleep time doing work. This would result in a better standard of work overall.

> *"You know you're maturing when sleep feels less like a punishment and more like a reward."*

This is a quote I believe resonates with many teens. We should work towards ensuring that we can achieve that reward. In the long run, and also possibly in the very near future, it will be very beneficial.

Get Enough Sleep

How does sleep help with time management? Getting enough sleep and quality sleep allows your brain to function better. As a result, you are more focused.

4

BUILD YOUR SOCIAL CIRCLE

"In fact, the socialization gives us the tools to fill our evolutionary roles. They are our building blocks."

—*Warren Farrel*

The importance of being social can be underestimated. I am not saying you should be personal friends with half of the world's population, but you need to build your communication skills. Building your social circle means diversifying your surroundings. Your beliefs should not sway and be influenced by the people you are surrounded by, but you should be able to communicate with people.

There will always be someone or some people who don't like you for whatever reason. You have no control over that. However, along with your closest friends, you must develop yourself in such a way that you are recognized by many. People should be able to trust you. People should be willing to help you. You should be able to call on almost anyone and they are not lost as to why you are communicating with them. When you build your social circle, if you find yourself in a situation where you are strapped for time, you can ask people for help. For example, you could have two tests one day and something to be printed. You studied in the morning and did not eat breakfast. You had two breaks at school. In the first break, you studied for the second test. In the second break, you needed to get the thing printed. Maybe the place to get it printed was busy that day because a lot of people had things to print. Knowing you had not eaten yet, you found someone you knew, someone who is not even a close friend—you don't even talk to them every day, but you knew each other and exchanged greetings once in a while—and you asked them if they could print it for you so you can go get something to eat. They said they would, and you emailed it to them and went to get food. Now that is a tiny example of a need to call on someone, and this example may not apply to everyone. People generally need to ask for help once in a while. If you had not socialised at all, you probably would not have had anyone you could have asked. Furthermore, you may not just want to ask anybody.

Another reason to build your social circle is to expand your knowledge. That may seem confusing. How is building your social circle going to expand your knowledge? Well, you get to hear new perspectives. This shouldn't sway your beliefs, but at least you can understand other perspectives. This is very useful when it comes to communication. Think about it, if you don't know how other people think, how can you communicate with them in a way they will understand? If you don't know the type of environment you are in, how will you adapt to it? You may be wondering how that helps with time management. This is mostly applicable to passion projects but can also apply to general communication. When you have a passion project and are trying to push your product or service to someone else, you need to know what your target audience is attracted to. So, surrounding yourself with people in your target audience will allow you to market better. You can save a lot of time and save yourself from a lot of stress when you already know what your target audience is looking for instead of doing a lot of research and guessing and having to readjust constantly when you realise one tactic is not working. For general communication, it spares you from arguments and misinterpretation. Imagine how much time you could get back if you knew how to communicate in such a way that the person on the receiving end understands. As a result, you would spend less time deliberating over misinterpretation and re-explanation. It could also spare unnecessary conflict. You can use that time to do something else that is more crucial. It may not seem like much, but it is the little things that make the difference.

5

TAKE A BREAK

"There is virtue in work and there is virtue in rest. Use both and overlook neither."

—*Alan Cohen*

All work and no play make Jack a dull boy, but all play and no work make Jack a mere toy. Work is useless if you never rest. Why? Your brain needs rest to function at full capacity. Often, after going through the process of procrastination, you decide to tackle everything at once. This may lead to a 5-hour or more work session without any breaks.

Procrastination is not a good thing, but if you don't take a break, that five hours is useless. By the end of that work session, it is likely that you are very tired and possibly only remember what you reviewed for the first hour, if so much, of your studying or the task you did in your work session took longer to do because you are not fully focused. This is why study methods like the Pomodoro Method are so popular. You don't necessarily have to take a break every twenty-five minutes like in the Pomodoro Method, but you definitely need a break when your brain stops focusing. This should not be used as an excuse to stop working every two minutes because your brain is not focused. You need to get focused first. Then when you are focused, and you start to lose your focus, you take a break. This is when things get tricky.

A break doesn't necessarily mean you are going to do something that is 'entertaining.' It just means you are going to take a break from studying or whichever task you are trying to focus on at that moment. In fact, I do not recommend using your breaks to go on social media or do any other form of entertainment. I recommend doing tasks that take a really short period of time to do; tasks that will take your brain off the main task but will remove things from your to-do list. For example, washing dishes. The aim is to take a brain break from that task, but the end goal is to maximise your time. One way to do that is to do anything that takes about five minutes or less to get done whenever you have the opportunity. This is why it is good to still have a to-do list, even if you have a schedule. You don't want to spend your break figuring out what to do, or you may end up on your phone. Once you get on your phone, it will be hard to get off. This can lead to wasting the rest of your focus session. This is bad news if your focus session is studying at the last minute for a test.

On the other hand, if you have nothing else to do besides what your focus session is dedicated to, you should try to take a break and do nothing. Sometimes it is very beneficial to just do nothing at all and give your brain a break from even processing anything. Maybe just stretch or get a screen break if the task you are doing requires you to sit around a computer or some other technological device. Depending on the length of your break, you can even take a power nap. A power nap generally lasts ten to thirty minutes and is meant to be a short nap. You don't necessarily have to fall asleep, but close your eyes. Power naps help improve productivity, according to apollo247.com. According to verywellmind.com, power napping can even reduce stress, but it is crucial to set the time for your power nap so you know you won't drift into a deep sleep.

As a last option for what to do in your break, if you decide to go on your phone to check messages or engage in some form of entertainment, you must have self-control. It is very easy to get carried away. It may be better to just avoid it completely, but if you really decide to, you must be able to stop when you need to stop. It is not good to go through so much effort to get yourself to start a task, and when you take your break, you cannot continue. That is why it is encouraged to take short breaks and use your breaks in such a way as to allow you to get focused again immediately when your break is complete.

When you are deciding how long your focus sessions should be and how long your breaks should be, remember that if you are no longer focused, you should take a break, but don't take a break long enough that you decide not to return to your task or lose the motivation you had to do that task.

6

YOU ARE YOUR BIGGEST MOTIVATOR

"Let no one discourage your ambitious attitude. You don't need a fan club to achieve your goals. Be your own motivation."

—*Mama Zara*

If you have a goal, it is reasonable to assume that you are going to work towards achieving it. Many people strive off external validation. People can feel demotivated if others don't congratulate them on the hard work they are putting in. Others may not notice your labour, but that doesn't mean you are not working hard; it just means it is not necessarily seen.

You can't decide to give up because you are not being encouraged and motivated by others. You should motivate yourself and have discipline. Strive towards achieving your goal no matter what circumstance you are in. There are people who will not be there until it is time to say congratulations. Some may even get jealous or believe it was easy to get where you got. Only you and God truly know the work that you put in because even if you got help, at the end of the day, you did it. It is truly less about motivation and more about discipline to stick with a task. Whether you have discipline or not is rooted in why you stick with a task. If you are doing a task to get praise from others, then you are motivated by external factors. Therefore, when you stop receiving praise from others, you will stop the task. Whereas, if you are doing a task in order to better yourself or to see a positive change in the world or anything along those lines, you will most likely stick to it because it doesn't matter if you are being motivated by others or not. What you are working towards doesn't rely on people motivating you; it only relies on discipline and self-motivation.

Doing a task you love that you don't rely on others to praise you for can give you the energy and internal motivation to work on other tasks you may not be as fond of. In the end, having the discipline and internal motivation to stick to something aids in tasks being completed quicker as you will procrastinate less because you have the discipline to finish.

7

PRAYER

"A day without prayer is a day without blessing, and a life without prayer is a life without power."

—*Edwin Harvey*

The value of prayer is underestimated in this generation. Something key to remember is that God sees everything that is happening, and He knows what you are struggling with. He can help you through it. God puts us through trials to make us stronger and so that we can put greater trust in Him. He will be right there by your side during the trial.

"Count it all joy, my brothers, when you meet trials of various kinds, for you know that the testing of your faith produces steadfastness. And let steadfastness have its full effect, that you may be perfect and complete, lacking in nothing." (James 1:2-4 – ESV).

I can testify to the fact that when I am focused on God's Word, everything is better. I feel less stressed, and I feel like someone understands.

Even when it feels like no one around you understands the pain you are going through, God does. He doesn't give anyone more than they can handle because He knows that when we put our trust in Him, we will get through. If it feels overwhelming, just know that God gives the hardest battles to the strongest soldiers. Do not underestimate the power of prayer. It can move mountains; but as much as you pray, you should still work. Faith without works is dead (see James 2:14). You can't pray for an A and study for a C. You must study like you are trying to get an A and put the rest in God's hands. Then, give thanks. When you ask someone for something, you say, "Thank you." When you ask God for something, say, "Thank You." The aim is to be in constant communication with God and not just call Him when you need something.

Life becomes easier with prayer. In addition to knowing that God understands and can help you, you know that there is more to life than this. You may be wondering what I mean by that. In essence, life gets rough, but when you know about the salvation that is ahead, you know that joy comes in the morning.

"For his anger endureth but a moment; in his favour is life: Weeping may endure for a night, but joy comes in the morning." (Psalm 30:5 – KJV).

Matthew 6:19-21 says, *"Lay not up for yourselves treasures upon earth, where moth and rust doth corrupt, and where thieves break through and steal: but lay up for yourselves treasures in heaven, where neither moth nor rust doth corrupt, and where thieves do not break through nor steal: for where your treasure is, there will your heart be also." (KJV).*

There are treasures in heaven greater than silver or gold, so you don't have to worry. Yes, you must work hard. Yes, you must do well. However, there is more to life than this.

8

WORK SMARTER, NOT HARDER

"It's not the load that breaks you down, it's the way you carry it."

—*Lena Horne*

It is no secret that you can get more done in less time; it depends on how you do it. It is also no secret that you can work for hours on end and reap little results. This is why people are constantly searching for easier ways to do things. The number of people working online has increased because of this. It is easier and takes much less energy, and sometimes, you may even earn more.

> *"I choose a lazy person to do a hard job. Because a lazy person will find an easy way to do it."*
>
> —*Bill Gates*

From a teenage perspective, our largest workload is school. There are assignments and tests constantly rolling in, and the stress is immeasurable. My aim in this chapter is to introduce some of the study methods that work best for me and to also get a better understanding of how to tackle tasks. When I say tasks, I don't necessarily mean schoolwork but goals in general.

When you set a goal, you want to achieve it. You will do everything in your power to get there, if it is really something you want. I previously mentioned that you need to have determination and motivate yourself because that is how you will get there. You can have the biggest motivation, but with no determination and discipline, you will get nowhere. This is why many people with New Year's resolutions fall off before February. They did not have the discipline to continue working towards their goal.

One thing that is necessary to achieve your goal is breaking it into micro-goals. Yearly goals can be broken into monthly goals, monthly goals into weekly goals, and further into continuous daily achievements. According to the author of Atomic Habits, James Clear, if you get better by 1% each day, by the end of the year, you will be approximately 37 times better than at the beginning of the year. This can be represented as 1.01^{365}.

In relation to study methods, some of the best, I believe, are the Pomodoro Technique, the Blurting Method, and the Teaching Method. The Pomodoro Technique is meant to allow your brain to absorb and process information. If you study without any breaks in between, your brain will become cluttered, and you will also become overwhelmed trying to remember so much information. Essentially, you keep adding more information to your brain before it gets a chance to process what has already been inputted.

The Blurting Method and the Teaching Method are similar but not the same. They are forms of active recall. In the blurting method, you write down everything you remember, and then you go back through the resources you have and write down— preferably in a different colour ink to differentiate— everything you forgot. This method of studying allows you to save information in your long-term memory as you are actively testing yourself. In this way, you can actually get an idea of what you remember. By repeating this process over and over, eventually, you will remember most if not everything you are trying to study. Every time you repeat this process, you are actively trying to remember something you did not remember the previous time.

On the other hand, the Teaching Method is literally turning yourself into a teacher. You would try to explain a concept you want to understand to someone else. It seems very simple at face value to just explain a concept to someone else, but when you start to analyse how this really works, you see its benefits. When you try to explain something to someone else, you want to think of it in the simplest way possible in order to make sure they understand. By doing this, you help yourself to understand the concept better as well.

The three study methods I just listed are some of the best I have found, but they are not the only ones that can be useful. It is also useful to tie what you want to know with what you already know. Making connections between different subjects and topics and connecting the concepts you are trying to understand with the real world will help you understand better.

Lastly, create questions while you study and answer them later. Making mock questions helps you to anticipate what will be in an upcoming assessment. This study method is also a form of active recall. By answering questions on a topic, you force your brain to remember information, thereby allowing you to actually learn instead of just reading without retaining it.

Never underestimate the power of a good study method because you get value for the time you spend studying. You could read for three hours straight and not remember anything. That is why you work smarter, not harder; not that you shouldn't work hard, but if you don't do it in an efficient way, you will not reap as many benefits.

9

SELF-CONTROL

"You need self-control in an out-of-control world."

—*James C. Collins*

"*Time flies when you're having fun*" is a very common phrase. Well, truly, time flies when you are on constant hits of dopamine. Let me explain. Dopamine is a compound present in the body as a neurotransmitter and a precursor of other substances, including adrenaline. Well, that is the definition you get when you look up the definition of dopamine on Google. Basically, dopamine allows you to feel pleasure or satisfaction. So, when you feel good about something, it is because you have a surge of dopamine in your brain. But what happens when your brain releases too much dopamine? Well, before answering that question, I should establish some of the things that release dopamine in the brain.

According to intoactionrecovery.com, high levels of dopamine are caused by actions such as drinking, drugs, gambling, playing video games, or using social media. This excitement leads us to continue these actions, leading to addiction. These activities give us instant hits of dopamine, and since you do not necessarily have to work very hard to release this dopamine, you keep going back for more. As stated before, this can lead to addiction and is the reason people have alcohol and drug addictions, and why when you are scrolling on social media, it is hard to stop; you keep wanting to go back to it. This is also why when your phone is taken away from you, you feel like you are going to "die." It is an addiction. Nothing I have just stated is my revelation, but rather a re-iteration of what research has already proven.

- Dopamine: the reason you would rather scroll than study.

- Dopamine: the reason you always want to listen to music.

- Dopamine: the reason junk food is so appealing.

Don't get me wrong, dopamine isn't 'bad.' Dopamine is also released when you are happy about a good grade, but the reason you do not want to study is that you rather have dopamine hits quickly and instantly. Too much of it is bad; just like many other things in life. Proper levels of dopamine are good.

When you are high on dopamine, it causes you to constantly go back to habits, whether they are beneficial or not. When someone takes a dopamine detox, they stop themselves from participating in possibly addictive activities, usually activities they see themselves getting addicted to. This allows someone to take control over their behaviour and develop improved emotional regulation and impulse control, according to psychcentral.com. This is self-control, which is the ability to control oneself, in particular, one's emotions and desires, especially in difficult situations.

Self-control helps you resist temptations, whether the temptation is to scroll or do something else. Ultimately, self-control gives you your time back. It gives you the ability to say to yourself, *"I've been scrolling for half an hour. I should stop,"* and then proceed to actually stop and do something important.

Self-control allows you to wake up in the morning and not open social media as a reflex but 'actually' start your day first. Self-control allows you to put down your phone an hour before bed to give your eyes a screen break to allow yourself to fall asleep properly. Time management cannot exist without self-control. You can never manage your time properly if you are not able to refrain from activities that are wasting your time. After all, time management is about balancing your time. The inability to control yourself and stop yourself from spending too much time on one task will cause imbalance. If you can't stop yourself from scrolling all day to allow time to do more important tasks, there is no time balance. If a task that seems as simple as that is something you cannot do, managing your time will be ultimately impossible.

IO

FULFILL YOUR PURPOSE, PURSUE YOUR PASSION

"Allow your passion to become your purpose, and it will one day become your profession."

—*Gabrielle Bernstein*

Never let your day get so busy with tasks that you don't do something you love. When you do something you love, it helps to refresh your mind. If you only do tasks that you are required to do and you don't necessarily like, the days will feel monotonous, boring, and stressful.

You should be joyful all the time, but you won't necessarily be happy or feel like there is something worth getting up for if you don't have something that you want to do. Yes, you get up, and yes, you have things that you will do because you must, but are any of those things something that you love to do?

Not only is doing something you love refreshing, but it can also lead to your purpose. They say when your job is something you love, you will never work a day in your life. That may be true if you continue to love it, but it goes beyond that. Passion, in this context, refers to an intense desire or enthusiasm for something. You can have a passion for painting. You could also have a passion for coding or maybe constructing. You could have a passion for designing, video creation, and teaching, and the list could go on and fill a book on its own. The point is, there are many things you can have a passion for, and everyone has a passion for something, even if you don't know what it is yet. Your passion can even have a direct correlation to a talent you may have.

A passion is something you love. It is something that if you got the opportunity to spend most of your time doing, you would probably do it, which is why, for some, it can turn out to be their purpose.

- Purpose: A person's sense of resolve or determination.

Your purpose and passion are things you must make time for, even in your busy schedule. It will benefit you in the long run, and it helps you serve others, which is ultimately something to strive for.

Having a passion to dedicate your time to every day not only motivates you to do other things but it gives you a reason to wake up every morning and it puts meaning behind all the effort you put in to manage your time effectively.

> *"Your passion is for you and your purpose is for others. When you use your passion in the service of others, it becomes your purpose."*
>
> *—Jay Shetty*

ABOUT THE AUTHOR

Tori Senior is currently a high school student in Jamaica. Although a lover of reading, she loves Mathematics. She is passionate about making the most of her time and loves participating in many activities. When she is not playing her instrument, the violin, she's making a splash in the pool.

Tori is passionate about helping others make the most of their time and have a less stressful life. She is determined to encourage others to pursue their passions and not be discouraged by the daily activities that demand their time.